SPORTS RECORDS

THE GREATEST BASEBALL RECORDS

BY MATT DOEDEN

CONSULTANT:

Craig R. Coenen, PhD
Associate Professor of History
Mercer County Community College
West Windsor, New Jersey

Capstone
press®
Mankato, Minnesota

Edge Books are published by Capstone Press,
151 Good Counsel Drive, P.O. Box 669, Mankato, Minnesota 56002.
www.capstonepress.com

Library of Congress Cataloging-in-Publication Data
Doeden, Matt.
    The greatest baseball records / by Matt Doeden.
    p. cm. — (Edge books. Sports records)
    Summary: "Short stories and tables of statistics describe the history and greatest
records of Major League Baseball" — Provided by publisher.
    Includes bibliographical references and index.
    ISBN-13: 978-1-4296-2005-5 (hardcover)
    ISBN-10: 1-4296-2005-6 (hardcover)
    1. Baseball — Records — United States — Juvenile literature. I. Title. II. Series.
GV877.D64 2009
796.357 — dc22   2008002030

Editorial Credits
Aaron Sautter, editor; Bobbi J. Wyss, designer; Jo Miller, photo researcher

Photo Credits
AP Images, 6, 8, 24; Denis Paquin, 4; James A. Finley, 7
Getty Images Inc./AFP/John G. Mabanglo, 10; AFP/Matt Campbell, 20; Bruce Bennett
    Studios, 28; Focus on Sport, 12; MLB Photos/Ron Vesely, cover (bottom right), 26;
    MLB Photos/National Baseball Hall of Fame Library, 16; Sportschrome/Rob Tringali,
    cover (top left); Sports Imagery/Ronald C. Modra, 14; Time Life Pictures/Hy Peskin, 22;
    Transcendental Graphics/Mark Rucker, 18
Shutterstock/Dewitt, cover (middle right); Marie C. Fields, cover (top right); Mike
    Flippo, cover (bottom left)

**Records in this book are from baseball's "modern era" beginning in 1903,
and are current through the 2007 season.**

1 2 3 4 5 6 13 12 11 10 09 08

TABLE OF CONTENTS

CHAPTER 1
PLAY BALL!   4

CHAPTER 2
BASEBALL'S GREATEST PLAYERS   8

CHAPTER 3
BASEBALL'S GREATEST TEAMS   16

CHAPTER 4
BASEBALL'S WILDEST RECORDS   22

GLOSSARY   30
READ MORE   31
INTERNET SITES   31
INDEX   32

PLAY BALL!

THE SUN

2 1 3 1

LEGG MASON

Bud

Coca-Cola

HIT I'st HERE

4

LEARN ABOUT

- Ripken's Record
- Baseball History
- The World Series

Cal Ripken Jr. is often called baseball's "Iron Man."

The crowd went wild as Baltimore Oriole Cal Ripken Jr. stepped onto the field on September 6, 1995. A huge banner bore the number 2,131. That was how many straight games Ripken had started. With this game, he would break the great Lou Gehrig's record of most **consecutive** games played.

The game became "official" in the fifth inning, meaning it couldn't be rained out. Ripken, known as the "Iron Man" of baseball, had achieved something many people thought would be impossible. He even topped the game off with a home run to help his team win. Ripken extended his famous run to 2,632 games before finally taking a game off in September 1998.

AMERICA'S PASTIME

Baseball has been the national pastime of the United States for more than 100 years. The National League started in 1876. The American League was formed in 1901. In 1903, the two leagues began playing the World Series to determine the world champion. That year marks the beginning of baseball's "modern era."

5

consecutive — when something happens several times in a row without a break

Jackie Robinson was the first African American major league player in the modern era.

The sport's popularity exploded in the 1920s. Stars like Ty Cobb and Babe Ruth drew thousands of fans to the game. In the 1940s, Jackie Robinson opened the door for African Americans to play in the major leagues. Robinson led the way for future stars like Hank Aaron, who broke Babe Ruth's home run record.

EDGE FACT

Record books once showed that Ty Cobb had 4,191 career hits. But research shows that he was given credit for a two-hit game twice in 1910. His total is now 4,189.

Early on, only 16 teams played for the world championship. But beginning in 1961, several new teams joined the league. Today, 30 teams compete for the prized World Series trophy. Current big league stars like Alex Rodriguez and Johan Santana carry on baseball's rich traditions. Each year, fans flock to games to watch these players and others try to set new baseball records.

Johan Santana has won several awards for his dominant pitching.

CHAPTER 2

BASEBALL'S
GREATEST PLAYERS

LEARN ABOUT

- Big-Time Hitters
- Dominant Pitchers
- Speedy Runners

Joe DiMaggio was one of the New York Yankees' greatest hitters.

56 IN A ROW

For New York Yankees fans, 1941 was all about outfielder Joe DiMaggio. DiMaggio had a hot streak that's unmatched in baseball history. Beginning May 15, DiMaggio got at least one hit in 56 straight games.

MOST CONSECUTIVE GAMES WITH A HIT

56	Joe DiMaggio	1941, New York Yankees
44	Pete Rose	1978, Cincinnati Reds
41	George Sisler	1922, St. Louis Browns
40	Ty Cobb	1911, Detroit Tigers
39	Paul Molitor	1987, Milwaukee Brewers

MOST CAREER HITS

4,256	Pete Rose	Cincinnati, Philadelphia, Montreal
4,189	Ty Cobb	Detroit, Philadelphia
3,771	Hank Aaron	Atlanta, Milwaukee
3,630	Stan Musial	St. Louis
3,514	Tris Speaker	Boston, Cleveland, Washington, Philadelphia

MOST HITS IN A SINGLE SEASON

262	Ichiro Suzuki	2004, Seattle Mariners
257	George Sisler	1920, St. Louis Browns
254	Francis O'Doul	1929, Philadelphia Phillies
254	Bill Terry	1930, New York Giants
253	Al Simmons	1925, Philadelphia Athletics

BEST CAREER BATTING AVERAGE

.366	Ty Cobb	Detroit, Philadelphia
.358	Rogers Hornsby	St. Louis, N.Y. Giants, Boston, Chicago Cubs
.356	Joe Jackson	Philadelphia, Cleveland, Chicago White Sox
.349	Pete Browning	Louisville, Cleveland, Pittsburgh, Cincinnati, St. Louis, Brooklyn
.346	Ed Delahanty	Philadelphia, Cleveland, Washington

Nobody has really come close to matching DiMaggio's historic hitting streak. Pete Rose hit in 44 straight games in 1978. That's impressive, but it's still almost two weeks short of what "Joltin' Joe" managed to do.

Barry Bonds' big swing has helped him break several home run records.

THE HOMER CHAMP

No slugger has hit more home runs than Barry Bonds. When he stepped to the plate on August 7, 2007, he was tied with Hank Aaron at 755 career homers. Washington Nationals' pitcher Mike Bacsik wound up and threw a fastball. Bonds took a big swing, and the ball sailed over the right-field fence. Bonds had just broken Aaron's record with 756 career homers.

It's not the only home run record Bonds owns. In 2001, he hit 73 homers in one season to break Mark McGwire's record of 70. Before McGwire, the record had belonged to Roger Maris. In 1961, Maris hit 61 homers to break Babe Ruth's old record of 60.

MOST HOME RUNS IN A SEASON

73	Barry Bonds	2001, San Francisco Giants
70	Mark McGwire	1998, St. Louis Cardinals
66	Sammy Sosa	1998, Chicago Cubs
65	Mark McGwire	1999, St. Louis Cardinals
64	Sammy Sosa	2001, Chicago Cubs

MOST CAREER HOME RUNS

762	Barry Bonds	Pittsburgh, San Francisco
755	Hank Aaron	Atlanta, Milwaukee
714	Babe Ruth	Boston, N.Y. Yankees
660	Willie Mays	N.Y./San Francisco Giants, N.Y. Mets
609	Sammy Sosa	Texas, Chicago, Baltimore

MOST RUNS BATTED IN (RBIs) IN A SEASON

191	Lewis Wilson	1930, Chicago Cubs
184	Lou Gehrig	1931, New York Yankees
183	Hank Greenberg	1937, Detroit Tigers
175	Jimmie Foxx	1938, Boston Red Sox
175	Lou Gehrig	1927, New York Yankees

MOST CAREER RUNS BATTED IN

2,297	Hank Aaron	Atlanta, Milwaukee
2,217	Babe Ruth	Boston, N.Y. Yankees
1,996	Barry Bonds	Pittsburgh, San Francisco
1,995	Lou Gehrig	N.Y. Yankees
1,991	Stan Musial	St. Louis

EDGE FACT

Recently, many people have begun questioning some baseball players' records. Several star players have been accused of using drugs called steroids to improve their performance. Steroids are believed to help a player throw a ball faster, hit a ball farther, and avoid injuries.

Orel Hershiser's dominant pitching led the Dodgers to the 1988 World Series title.

UNTOUCHABLE

In 1988, Los Angeles Dodger pitcher Orel Hershiser dominated batters like few others. He threw five straight **shutout** games that year. By the ninth inning of the season's final game, Hershiser had pitched 58 straight scoreless innings. It was enough to tie Don Drysdale's previous record. But the game was tied and went into extra innings. Hershiser kept hurling the ball. By the end of the game, Hershiser had set a new record of 59 straight scoreless innings.

shutout — when a team doesn't score

MOST CONSECUTIVE SHUTOUT INNINGS

59.0	Orel Hershiser	1988, Los Angeles Dodgers
58.2	Don Drysdale	1968, Los Angeles Dodgers
55.2	Walter Johnson	1913, Washington Senators
53.0	Jack Coombs	1910, Philadelphia Athletics
47.0	Bob Gibson	1968, St. Louis Cardinals

MOST STRIKEOUTS IN A SEASON (PITCHING)

383	Nolan Ryan	1973, California Angels
382	Sandy Koufax	1965, Los Angeles Dodgers
372	Randy Johnson	2001, Arizona Diamondbacks
367	Nolan Ryan	1974, California Angels
364	Randy Johnson	1999, Arizona Diamondbacks

MOST CAREER STRIKEOUTS (PITCHING)

5,714	Nolan Ryan	N.Y. Mets, California, Houston, Texas
4,672	Roger Clemens	Boston, Toronto, N.Y. Yankees, Houston
4,616	Randy Johnson	Montreal, Seattle, Houston, Arizona, N.Y. Yankees
4,136	Steve Carlton	St. Louis, Philadelphia, San Francisco, Chicago, Cleveland, Minnesota
3,701	Bert Blyleven	Minnesota, Texas, Pittsburgh, Cleveland, California

MOST SAVES IN A SEASON

57	Bobby Thigpen	1990, Chicago White Sox
55	Eric Gagne	2003, Los Angeles Dodgers
55	John Smoltz	2002, Atlanta Braves
53	Trevor Hoffman	1998, San Diego Padres
53	Randy Myers	1993, Chicago Cubs
53	Mariano Rivera	2004, New York Yankees

MOST CAREER SAVES

524	Trevor Hoffman	Florida, San Diego
478	Lee Smith	Chicago Cubs, Boston, St. Louis, N.Y. Yankees, Baltimore, California, Cincinnati, Montreal
443	Mariano Rivera	N.Y. Yankees
424	John Franco	Cincinnati, N.Y. Mets, Houston
390	Dennis Eckersley	Cleveland, Boston, Chicago Cubs, Oakland, St. Louis

MOST CAREER WINS

511	Cy Young	Cleveland, St. Louis, Boston
417	Walter Johnson	Washington
373	Grover Alexander	Philadelphia, Chicago, St. Louis
373	Christy Mathewson	N.Y. Giants, Cincinnati
363	Warren Spahn	Boston, Milwaukee, N.Y. Mets, San Francisco

Rickey Henderson's blazing speed helped him set several base-running records.

PRINCE OF THIEVES

Stealing bases is a skill mastered by few baseball players. And nobody was better at it than Rickey Henderson. In 1982, the speedy Henderson had already stolen 84 bases by the **All-Star break**. By August 26, he was tied with Lou Brock's record of 118 in a season. On August 27, Henderson smashed the record by stealing four bases against the Milwaukee Brewers. Henderson went on to steal a record 130 bases that season and a record 1,406 in his career.

All-Star break — a break at the halfway point of the season when baseball's biggest stars play in the All-Star game

MOST STOLEN BASES IN A SEASON

130	Rickey Henderson	1982, Oakland Athletics
118	Lou Brock	1974, St. Louis Cardinals
110	Vince Coleman	1985, St. Louis Cardinals
109	Vince Coleman	1987, St. Louis Cardinals
108	Rickey Henderson	1983, Oakland Athletics

MOST CAREER STOLEN BASES

1,406	Rickey Henderson	Oakland, N.Y. Yankees, Toronto, San Diego, Anaheim, N.Y. Mets, Seattle, Boston, Los Angeles
938	Lou Brock	Chicago Cubs, St. Louis
892	Ty Cobb	Detroit, Philadelphia
808	Tim Raines	Montreal, Chicago White Sox, N.Y. Yankees, Oakland, Baltimore, Florida
752	Vince Coleman	St. Louis, N.Y. Mets, Kansas City, Seattle, Cincinnati, Detroit

MOST RUNS SCORED IN A SEASON

177	Babe Ruth	1921, New York Yankees
167	Lou Gehrig	1936, New York Yankees
163	Lou Gehrig	1931, New York Yankees
163	Babe Ruth	1928, New York Yankees
158	Chuck Klein	1930, Philadelphia Phillies
158	Babe Ruth	1920, New York Yankees
158	Babe Ruth	1927, New York Yankees

MOST CAREER RUNS SCORED

2,295	Rickey Henderson	Oakland, N.Y. Yankees, Toronto, San Diego, Anaheim, N.Y. Mets, Seattle, Boston, Los Angeles
2,246	Ty Cobb	Detroit, Philadelphia
2,227	Barry Bonds	Pittsburgh, San Francisco
2,174	Hank Aaron	Atlanta, Milwaukee
2,174	Babe Ruth	Boston, N.Y. Yankees

EDGE FACT

Pitcher Jim Kaat and third baseman Brooks Robinson share a defensive record. They each won a career-high 16 Gold Glove awards as the best fielders at their positions.

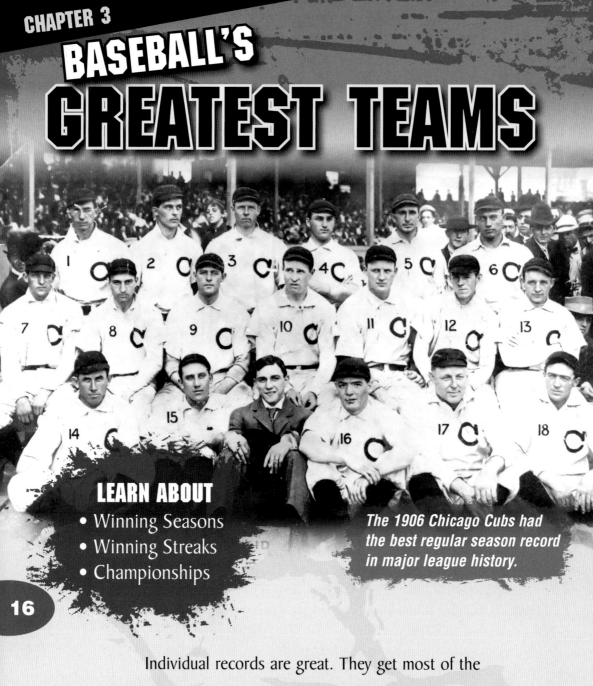

CHAPTER 3

BASEBALL'S
GREATEST TEAMS

LEARN ABOUT
- Winning Seasons
- Winning Streaks
- Championships

The 1906 Chicago Cubs had the best regular season record in major league history.

16

Individual records are great. They get most of the
attention from fans and the media. But baseball is a
team game. And for the team, it's all about winning.

BEST WINNING PERCENTAGE IN A SEASON

.763 (116-36)	Chicago Cubs	1906
.741 (103-36)	Pittsburgh Pirates	1902
.724 (110-42)	Pittsburgh Pirates	1909
.721 (111-43)	Cleveland Indians	1954
.716 (116-46)	Seattle Mariners	2001

MOST WINS TO START A SEASON

13	Milwaukee Brewers	1987
13	Atlanta Braves	1982
11	Oakland Athletics	1981
10	Brooklyn Dodgers	1955
10	Pittsburgh Pirates	1962
10	Cleveland Indians	1966

RACKING UP THE WINS

The 1906 Chicago Cubs were the best regular season team in baseball history. The Cubs crushed the competition that season, going 116-36. The team won more than three out of every four games!

In 2001, the Seattle Mariners matched Chicago's win total, but needed 10 more games to do it. They finished the season at 116-46. Strangely, neither of these two historic teams won the World Series after their regular season success.

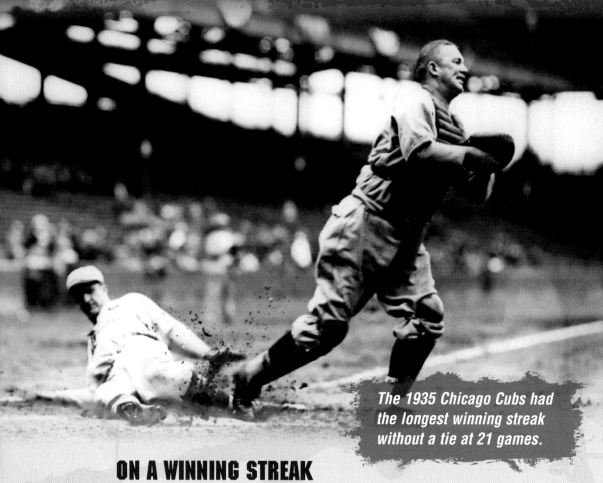

The 1935 Chicago Cubs had the longest winning streak without a tie at 21 games.

ON A WINNING STREAK

The 1916 New York Giants had the longest winning **streak** in baseball history. Their 26-game winning streak is especially interesting because they needed 27 games to do it. How is that possible? In the early days, baseball was only played during the day. If the score was tied at sunset, the game ended in a tie. The Giants had a tie game in the middle of their streak. Baseball doesn't count ties, so the Giants get credit for a 26-game winning streak.

streak — an unbroken series of games

LONGEST WINNING STREAKS

26	New York Giants	1916
21	Chicago Cubs	1935
20	Oakland Athletics	2002
19	Chicago White Sox	1906
19	New York Yankees	1947

TEAM SCORING RECORDS

Most runs in a season:	1,067	New York Yankees	1931
Most runs in a game:	30	Texas Rangers	2007
Most runs in an inning:	17	Boston Red Sox	1953

TEAM HITTING RECORDS

Most hits in a season:	1,783	Philadelphia Phillies	1930
Most hits in a game:	33	Cleveland Indians	1932
Most home runs in a season:	264	Seattle Mariners	1997
Highest batting average in a season:	.319	New York Giants	1930

TEAM PITCHING RECORDS

Fewest runs allowed in a season:	379	Chicago Cubs	1906
Lowest Earned Run Average in a season:	1.73	Chicago Cubs	1907
Most strikeouts in a season:	1,404	Chicago Cubs	2003
Most saves in a season:	68	Chicago White Sox	1990

EDGE FACT

On August 22, 2007, the Texas Rangers trailed the Baltimore Orioles 3-0. Then they exploded for 30 runs, the most ever scored in a major league game.

The New York Yankees have won more World Series titles than any other major league team.

WINNING IT ALL

Every fan and player knows that winning the World Series is what it's all about. Just ask Chicago Cubs fans — their team hasn't won a title since 1908! Chicago's drought is the longest in baseball history.

MOST WORLD SERIES TITLES

26	New York Yankees	1923, 1927–28, 1932, 1936–39, 1941, 1943, 1947, 1949–53, 1956, 1958, 1961–62, 1977–78, 1996, 1998–2000
10	St. Louis Cardinals	1926, 1931, 1934, 1942, 1944, 1946, 1964, 1967, 1982, 2006
9	Philadelphia/Oakland Athletics	1910–11, 1913, 1929–30, 1972–74, 1989
7	Boston Red Sox	1903, 1912, 1915–16, 1918, 2004, 2007
6	Brooklyn/Los Angeles Dodgers	1955, 1959, 1963, 1965, 1981, 1988

WORLD SERIES RECORDS

Most home runs in a World Series:	**14**	San Francisco Giants	2002
Most runs in a World Series:	**55**	New York Yankees	1960
Most runs in a World Series game:	**18**	New York Giants	1936
Most hits in a World Series:	**91**	New York Yankees	1960
Most hits in a World Series game:	**22**	Arizona Diamondbacks	2001

The New York Yankees, on the other hand, know a thing or two about winning championships. No other team comes close to matching the Yankees' 26 World Series titles. The Yankees also hold the record for consecutive World Series wins. They won five titles in a row from 1949 to 1953.

EDGE FACT

From 1995 to 2005, the Atlanta Braves won their division 11 years in a row. It's a record that may never be matched.

CHAPTER 4

BASEBALL'S
WILDEST RECORDS

LEARN ABOUT

- The Smallest Player
- Losing Streaks
- The Longest Game

Eddie Gaedel's small size made him almost impossible to strike out.

Records for home runs, strikeouts, and stolen bases are fun. But there are some records few fans have ever heard about. Baseball is filled with many wild and interesting records.

HEIGHT AND AGE

Shortest player:	Eddie Gaedel	3 feet, 7 inches (1.1 meters)
Tallest player:	Jon Rauch	6 feet, 11 inches (2.1 meters)
Youngest player:	Joe Nuxhall	15 years, 10 months, 11 days
Oldest player:	Satchel Paige	59 years, 2 months, 18 days

FIRSTS AND LASTS

Player to hit four home runs in a game:

First:	Lou Gehrig	1936
Last:	Carlos Delgado	2003

Player to hit two grand slams in one game:

First:	Tony Lazzeri	1936
Last:	Bill Mueller	2003

Player to turn an unassisted triple play:

First:	Neal Ball	1909
Last:	Troy Tulowitzki	2007

ANYONE CAN PLAY

The great thing about baseball is that, big or small, almost anyone can play the game. Eddie Gaedel was the shortest player in major league history. He stood just 3 feet, 7 inches (1.1 meters) tall. Gaedel wore the number "1/8" and had one plate appearance for the St. Louis Browns in 1951. Because he was so small, he had the smallest **strike zone** in baseball history. It's no surprise that Gaedel was walked on just four pitches.

23

strike zone — the area above home plate between a batter's knees and shoulders

ANOTHER KIND OF STREAK

Every team starts a new season hoping for success.
But that hope died quickly for the 1988 Baltimore
Orioles. The team lost the first 21 games of the season!
The team fired its manager after just six losses. But
even that drastic move didn't help. The Orioles still
ended up with the worst start in league history.

The 1988 Baltimore Orioles
had the worst start to a
season in league history.

LONGEST LOSING STREAKS

23 GAMES	Philadelphia Phillies	1961
21 GAMES	Baltimore Orioles	1988
20 GAMES	Boston Red Sox	1906
20 GAMES	Philadelphia Athletics	1916
20 GAMES	Philadelphia Athletics	1943
20 GAMES	Montreal Expos	1969

WORST WINNING PERCENTAGE IN A SEASON

.235 (36-117)	Philadelphia Athletics	1916
.248 (38-115)	Boston Braves	1935
.250 (40-120)	New York Mets	1962
.251 (38-113)	Washington Senators	1904
.265 (43-119)	Detroit Tigers	2003

The Orioles' losing streak was the worst to start a season, but it's not the worst overall. In 1961, the Philadelphia Phillies lost an amazing 23 games in a row. The team went almost a whole month without a single win.

EDGE FACT

The Minnesota Twins celebrated their first World Series title in 1987. But they were far from dominating. In the regular season, they went just 85-77. No team has ever lost so many games and still won a championship.

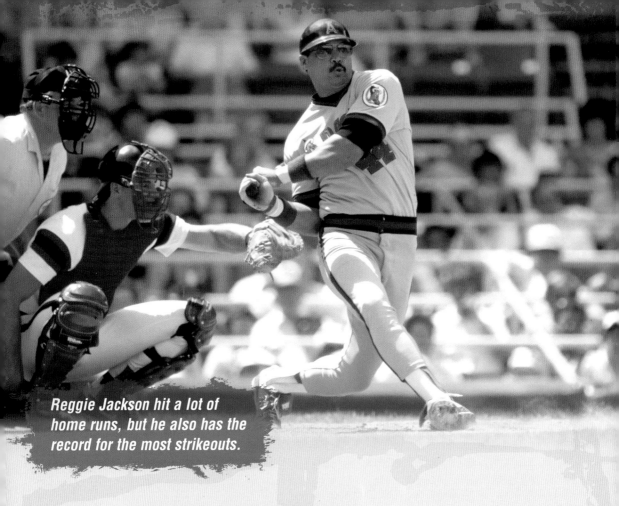

Reggie Jackson hit a lot of home runs, but he also has the record for the most strikeouts.

RECORDS NOBODY WANTS

Big-time hitters often end up striking out more often than they hit the ball. Who holds the record for being struck out the most? That honor goes to Reggie Jackson. Jackson was a great hitter who smashed 563 career homers from 1967 to 1987. But his big, all-or-nothing swing also led to a record 2,597 strikeouts.

MOST CAREER STRIKEOUTS (AT BAT)

2,597	Reggie Jackson	Oakland, Baltimore, N.Y. Yankees, California
2,306	Sammy Sosa	Texas, Chicago White Sox, Chicago Cubs, Baltimore
2,043	Jim Thome	Cleveland, Philadelphia, Chicago White Sox
2,003	Andrés Galarraga	Montreal, St. Louis, Colorado, Atlanta, Texas, San Francisco, Anaheim
1,942	Jose Canseco	Oakland, Texas, Boston, Toronto, Tampa Bay, N.Y. Yankees, Anaheim, Chicago White Sox, Montreal, Los Angeles

MOST TIMES HIT BY A PITCH

285	Craig Biggio	Houston
267	Don Baylor	Baltimore, Oakland, California, N.Y. Yankees, Boston, Minnesota
243	Ron Hunt	N.Y. Mets, Los Angeles, San Francisco, Montreal, St. Louis
218	Jason Kendall	Pittsburgh, Oakland, Chicago Cubs, Milwaukee
198	Frank Robinson	Cincinnati, Baltimore, Los Angeles, California, Cleveland

MOST CAREER HOME RUNS ALLOWED

505	Robin Roberts	Philadelphia, Baltimore, Houston, Chicago Cubs
484	Fergie Jenkins	Philadelphia, Chicago Cubs, Texas, Boston
482	Phil Niekro	Atlanta, N.Y. Yankees, Cleveland, Toronto
472	Don Sutton	Los Angeles, Houston, Milwaukee, Oakland, California
448	Frank Tanana	California, Boston, Texas, Detroit, N.Y. Mets, N.Y. Yankees

MOST WALKS ALLOWED IN A SEASON

208	Bob Feller	1938, Cleveland Indians
204	Nolan Ryan	1977, California Angels
202	Nolan Ryan	1974, California Angels
194	Bob Feller	1941, Cleveland Indians
192	Bobo Newsom	1938, St. Louis Browns

MOST LOSSES BY A PITCHER

316	Cy Young	Cleveland, St. Louis, Boston
292	Nolan Ryan	N.Y. Mets, California, Houston, Texas
279	Walter Johnson	Washington
274	Phil Niekro	Atlanta, N.Y. Yankees, Cleveland, Toronto
265	Gaylord Perry	San Francisco, Cleveland, Texas, San Diego, N.Y. Yankees, Atlanta, Seattle, Kansas City

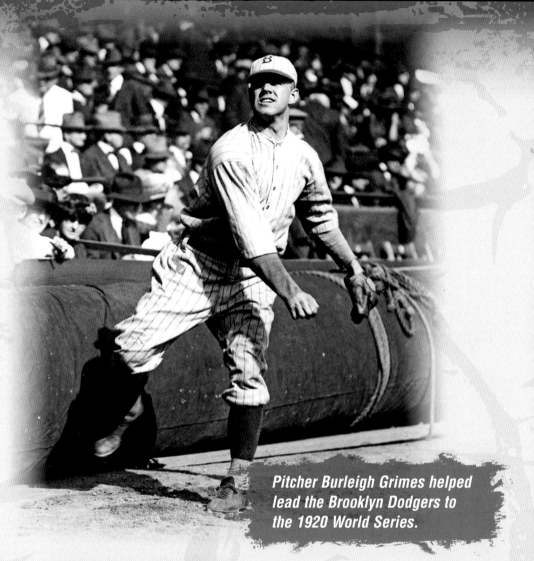

Pitcher Burleigh Grimes helped lead the Brooklyn Dodgers to the 1920 World Series.

WORKING OVERTIME

Nine innings isn't enough for some games. On May 1, 1920, it took 26 innings to finish a game between the Brooklyn Dodgers and the Boston Braves. It was the longest game in major league history. Boston pitcher Joe Oeschger threw 20 straight shutout innings, but couldn't get the win. The game was finally called off due to darkness. It ended in a 1-1 tie.

MOST INNINGS PLAYED IN A GAME

26	Brooklyn Dodgers 1, Boston Braves 1	May 1, 1920
25	St. Louis Cardinals 4, New York Mets 3	September 11, 1974
25	Chicago White Sox 7, Milwaukee Brewers 6	May 8, 1984
24	Detroit Tigers 1, Philadelphia Athletics 1	July 21, 1945
24	Houston Astros 1, New York Mets 0	April 15, 1968

HIGHEST HOME ATTENDANCE IN A SEASON

4,483,350	Colorado Rockies	1993
4,271,867	New York Yankees	2007
4,200,518	New York Yankees	2006
4,090,692	New York Yankees	2005
4,057,947	Toronto Blue Jays	1993
4,028,318	Toronto Blue Jays	1992
3,891,014	Colorado Rockies	1996

The Dodgers then lost their next two games in a total of 32 innings. The Dodgers set a second major league record that year by playing 58 innings in just three games! The practice must have helped, though, because the Dodgers made it all the way to the World Series that season.

Baseball's greatest records aren't just about numbers. They're about the men and teams who achieved something nobody has ever done. Great records don't just capture the fans' imaginations — they keep fans coming back for more.

29

EDGE FACT

On October 8, 1956, Don Larson became the only pitcher in baseball history to throw a perfect game in the World Series. His performance led the Yankees to a 2-0 win over the Brooklyn Dodgers.

GLOSSARY

All–Star break (AWL-star BRAYK) — a break at the halfway point of the season when baseball's biggest stars play in the All-Star game

consecutive (kuhn-SEK-yuh-tiv) — when something happens several times in a row without a break

fastball (FAST-bawl) — a straight, fast pitch that often exceeds 90 miles (145 kilometers) per hour

Gold Glove (GOHLD GLUHV) — an award honoring the best fielder at each position in both the National and American leagues

modern era (MOD-urn IHR-uh) — the era of baseball from 1903 to the present

perfect game (PUR-fikt GAME) — a game in which a pitcher doesn't allow a single batter to reach first base

shutout (SHUHT-out) — when a team doesn't score

streak (STREEK) — an unbroken series of games

strike zone (STRIKE ZOHN) — the area above the home plate between a batter's knees and shoulders

READ MORE

Altergott, Hanna. *Great Teams in Baseball History.* Great Teams. Chicago: Raintree, 2006.

Buckley, James. *Baseball Top 10.* New York: DK, 2004.

Stewart, Mark and Mike Kennedy. *Long Ball: The Legend and Lore of the Home Run.* Minneapolis: Millbrook Press, 2006.

INTERNET SITES

FactHound offers a safe, fun way to find Internet sites related to this book. All of the sites on FactHound have been researched by our staff.

Here's how:
1. Visit *www.facthound.com*
2. Choose your grade level.
3. Type in this book ID **1429620056** for age-appropriate sites. You may also browse subjects by clicking on letters, or by clicking on pictures and words.
4. Click on the **Fetch It** button.

FactHound will fetch the best sites for you!

31

INDEX

Aaron, Hank, 6, 10
American League, 5
Atlanta Braves, 21

Baltimore Orioles, 24
Bonds, Barry, 10
Brooklyn Dodgers, 28–29

Chicago Cubs, 16, 17, 20
Cobb, Ty, 6

DiMaggio, Joe, 8–9
Drysdale, Don, 12

Gaedel, Eddie, 22, 23

Henderson, Rickey, 14
Hershiser, Orel, 12

Jackson, Reggie, 26

Maris, Roger, 10
McGwire, Mark, 10
Minnesota Twins, 25
MLB history, 5–7

National League, 5
New York Giants, 18
New York Yankees, 20, 21

Philadelphis Phillies, 25

records
    age, 23
    base stealing, 14–15
    batting averages, 9
    championships, 21
    consecutive games played, 5
    fielding, 15
    height, 23
    hitting, 6, 8–9
    home attendance, 29
    home runs, 10–11
    longest games, 28–29
    losing streaks, 24–25
    pitching, 12–13, 27, 29
    runs batted in, 11
    runs scored, 15
    strikeouts at bat, 26–27
    team hitting, 19
    team pitching, 19
    team scoring, 19
    winning percentages, 17, 25
    winning streaks, 18–19
    wins, 17
Ripken Jr., Cal, 4, 5
Robinson, Jackie, 6
Ruth, Babe, 6, 10

steroids, 11

World Series, 5, 7, 17, 20–21,
    25, 28, 29